Copyright © 2023 by Trient Press

All rights reserved. No part of this publication may be reproduced, distributed, or transmitted in any form or by any means, including photocopying, recording, or other electronic or mechanical methods, without the prior written permission of the publisher, except in the case of brief quotations embodied in critical reviews and certain other noncommercial uses permitted by copyright law. For permission requests, write to the publisher, addressed "Attention: Permissions Coordinator," at the address below.

Criminal copyright infringement, including infringement without monetary gain, is investigated by the FBI and is punishable by up to five years in federal prison and a fine of $250,000.

Except for the original story material written by the author, all songs, song titles, and lyrics mentioned in the novel From Data to Disruption: How AI is Changing Business Forever are the exclusive property of the respective artists, songwriters, and copyright holder.

Trient Press
3375 S Rainbow Blvd
#81710, SMB 13135
Las Vegas, NV 89180

Ordering Information:
Quantity sales. Special discounts are available on quantity purchases by corporations, associations, and others. For details, contact the publisher at the address above.
Orders by U.S. trade bookstores and wholesalers. Please contact Trient Press: Tel: (775) 996-3844; or visit www.trientpress.com.

Printed in the United States of America

Publisher's Cataloging-in-Publication data
Trient Press
A title of a book : Trientrepreneur

Now On

What's Your M.E.S.S ?

Hosted By
Tracey D. Armstrong

Special Guest
It could be You...

What's your M.E.S.S.?
Mental.Emotional.Social.Status. Takes you through the mess of successful people's lives and tells the backstory of when their Mental, Emotional, Social, Status of life was a complete mess and what they did to clean up the messes in their lives. .

TRIENT PRESS MINDSET MOMENTS MAGAZINE

---

05 Illuminating December: A Journey of Hope and Unity

07 Transformative Journeys: Winter Solstice Traditions Around the World

11 The Light of Kwanzaa: Principles for Building Hope and Unity

13 Lighting the Path: The Rennervation Foundation Mission of Hope and Purpose

18 December Reflections: Embracing the End as a New Beginning

MINDSET MOMENTS
ISSUE 2

19 Sacred Symbols: The Star of Bethlehem

22 The Art of Giving: Philanthropic Movements Making a difference This Holiday Season

24 December Affirmations

26 Festive Innovations: Sustainable and Eco-Friendly Holiday Practices

27 Embracing Resilience: Mindset Shift in the Face of Challenges

28 Cover Story: Deaunna Marie: The Holistic Visionary of our Times

30 Recipes

Editor-in-Chief
Head Staff-Writer
Melisa Ruscsak

Managing Editor
Graphic Design Editor
Kristina Wenzl-Figueroa

TRIENT PRESS MINDSET MOMENTS MAGAZINE   DECEMBER 2023

Trientrepreneur magazine

Elevate Your Brand to New Heights:
Your Face Could Grace Our Inspiring Cover!

 Follow our social networks

So, why wait? Take the leap, and let your brand's narrative intertwine with ours. Your journey towards innovation, leadership, and lasting impact begins with Trient Press Magazine. Your face on our cover could be the catalyst for a remarkable chapter in your brand's story.

Visit us at
www.treintpressmagazine.com

ILLUMINATING DECEMBER: A JOURNEY OF HOPE AND UNITY

Embracing the Season of Light: Daily Reflections on Hope
Begin each December day with a reflection on hope. In the midst of winter's darkness, let the concept of hope illuminate your thoughts, creating a sense of warmth and optimism.

Family Traditions: Strengthening Bonds in the Holiday Season
December is a time to fortify family connections. Whether it's through shared holiday preparations or cozy evenings by the fire, cherish these moments that knit the fabric of family life.

Meditation on Peace and Unity: Cultivating Inner Harmony
Incorporate meditations focusing on peace and unity into your daily routine. This practice fosters a feeling of togetherness and harmony, both within oneself and in the world.

Culinary Celebrations: Exploring Holiday Flavors
Delight in the culinary joys of December. From baking festive treats to preparing traditional holiday meals, these activities offer delicious ways to celebrate the season.

Journal of Reflections: Capturing December's Magic
Keep a journal throughout the month to chronicle your experiences and reflections. This practice allows you to capture the essence of December's magic and the lessons it brings.

Acts of Kindness: Spreading Joy and Compassion
In the spirit of the holiday season, engage in acts of kindness and compassion. Whether it's through charity work or small gestures of goodwill, these actions embody the essence of December's spirit.

Creating Meaningful Holiday Rituals
Establish personal holiday rituals that resonate with your beliefs and values. From lighting candles to commemorate the season's festivals to engaging in reflective conversations, these traditions add depth to your celebrations.

Celebrating Achievements: Reflecting on the Year's End
As the year draws to a close, take time to celebrate your personal and professional milestones. Reflect on the growth and the journeys undertaken, setting intentions for the year ahead.

Honoring Cultural Celebrations: Understanding Diverse Traditions
Explore and honor the various cultural celebrations that occur in December, such as Christmas, Hanukkah, and Kwanzaa. Understanding these traditions fosters a sense of global unity and respect.

Moments of Mindfulness: Embracing the Season's Serenity
Dedicate time each day for mindful contemplation. In the quiet of December, these moments of stillness allow for a deeper connection with the season's serene and hopeful essence.

" **Assembly of Wanderers**

Join us in navigating life's complexities, as we collectively shift from a reactive to a proactive mindset, replacing blame and expectation with gratitude and love, and realizing that within each of us lies the potential for unparalleled achievement, deep fulfillment, and a truly extraordinary quality of life.cumsan lacus vel facilisis.

FOR MORE INFORMATION VISIT: wandercon.assemblyofwanderers.com

Prepare to be inspired and transformed! Join us with a lineup of luminaries:
⭐ Master Trainer: Antonio T. Smith Jr.
🏈 Celebrity Speaker: Liffort Hobley
🎤 Keynote Maestros: Sheena Kerley, Deaunna Marie, Law Loadholt, and Tracey Armstrong.

An unparalleled assembly of brilliance awaits. Ensure your presence in this intellectual symposium—reserve swiftly, as seating is limited.

Awaken your spirit, and enhance the beauty within.

Instagram_ Account   Facebook_ Account   Twitter_ Account

Transformative Journeys: Celebrating Winter Solstice Traditions Around the World

"In the heart of winter's shadow, lies the promise of light. As the earth tilts away from the sun, we are reminded that every ending is but a prelude to a new beginning. Let the solstice be our guide, illuminating the path from darkness to renewal, where ancient stones whisper and global hearts unite in the dance of celestial harmony."

Embracing the Darkest Day: A Global Tapestry of Renewal and Introspection

As the Northern Hemisphere tilts furthest from the sun, the winter solstice marks the shortest day and the longest night of the year. Across cultures, this celestial event has been celebrated for millennia, not just as a marker of the winter season, but as a profound moment of transformation, renewal, and introspection. From the ancient stone circles of Europe to the lantern festivals of Asia, each tradition weaves a unique narrative around this astronomical phenomenon, reflecting deep-rooted beliefs and values.

The Ancient Stones Speak: Winter Solstice at Stonehenge, United Kingdom

In the rolling plains of Wiltshire, England, the prehistoric monument of Stonehenge stands as a testament to the astronomical knowledge of the ancients. During the winter solstice, these towering stones align perfectly with the setting sun, a spectacle that draws thousands each year. Historians and archaeologists speculate that for the Neolithic people, this alignment signified the death and rebirth of the sun, a moment to release the old and embrace the new. Today, visitors from around the globe gather at Stonehenge, participating in a tradition that transcends time, joining hands in a spirit of reverence and community.

The Festival of Light: Dongzhi, China

In China, the winter solstice is celebrated as Dongzhi, one of the most important festivals in the lunar calendar. This festival, deeply rooted in the philosophy of yin and yang, symbolizes the balance and harmony in life. Families come together to enjoy a feast, where the star is often tangyuan – sweet rice balls symbolizing reunion and completeness. In this simple act of sharing a meal, there is a powerful reminder of the interconnectedness of life and the importance of family bonds.

The Sun Stands Still: Yule in Scandinavian Tradition

Yule, a festival observed by the indigenous Germanic peoples, including the Norse and the Vikings, marks the winter solstice with a series of customs that celebrate the return of the sun. One of the most enduring symbols of Yule is the Yule log, a specially chosen log burned in the hearth, symbolizing warmth, light, and protection. The burning of the Yule log is a ritual of purification and a prayer for the sun's return, a poignant reminder of nature's cycles and our place within them.

"Embracing the Eternal Cycle: As the Yule log crackles in the heart of winter, we are reminded of ancient traditions that honor the enduring dance of light and darkness. In this moment, where the sun stands still, we find warmth in the promise of longer days ahead, a timeless celebration of nature's unending rhythm."

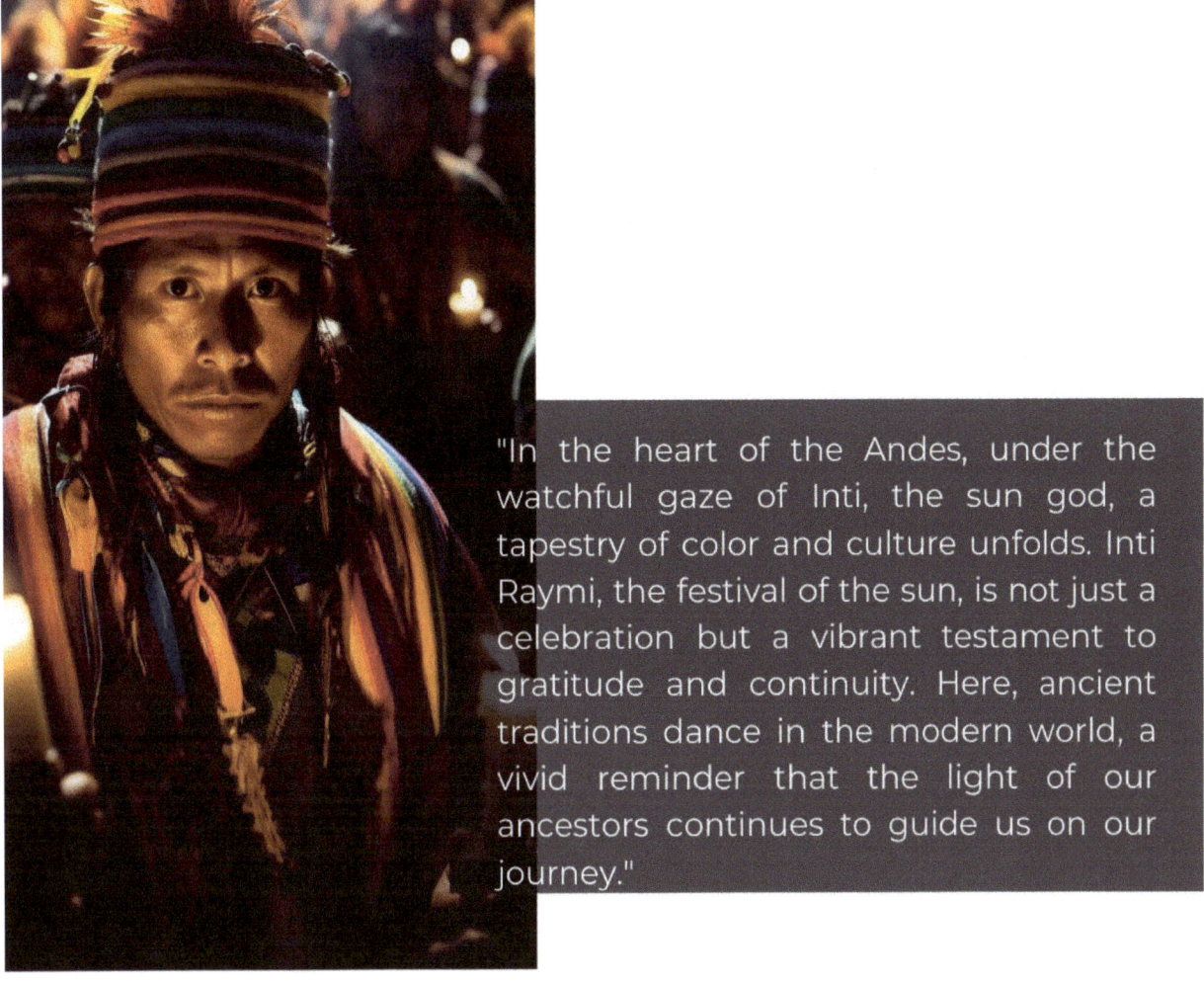

"In the heart of the Andes, under the watchful gaze of Inti, the sun god, a tapestry of color and culture unfolds. Inti Raymi, the festival of the sun, is not just a celebration but a vibrant testament to gratitude and continuity. Here, ancient traditions dance in the modern world, a vivid reminder that the light of our ancestors continues to guide us on our journey."

The Return of the Light: Inti Raymi in Peru

Far from the cold landscapes of Northern Europe, the Incas in Peru celebrated Inti Raymi, the festival of the sun. Although the original customs have evolved over time, modern celebrations still honor the sun god, Inti, with vibrant parades, colorful costumes, and traditional dances. This festival is a stirring display of gratitude to the sun, a life-giving force, and a reminder of the enduring presence of ancient cultures in our contemporary world.

Reflection and Renewal: A Universal Theme

These diverse traditions, while unique in their expressions, share common themes of reflection, renewal, and the celebration of light. The winter solstice invites us to pause, to look inward, and to contemplate the cycles of nature. It's a time to gather with loved ones, to share stories and warmth, and to prepare for the lengthening days ahead.

As we journey through these global traditions, we are reminded of our shared humanity and the universal quest for meaning, connection, and renewal. The winter solstice, in its quiet majesty, offers a moment of unity, an opportunity to celebrate not just the return of the light, but the light within us all.

Embark on a journey of wisdom and camaraderie at Dove and Dragon Radio. Tune in for riveting conversations spanning business strategies, travel tales, and more.

THE WORLD EVOLVES, RADIO TRANSFORMS.
WELCOME TO A NEW ERA OF AUDITORY EXPLORATION.

The Light of Kwanzaa: Seven Principles for Building Hope and Unity

Introduction:

Kwanzaa, a celebration of African-American culture and heritage, offers more than a week of festivity; it provides a blueprint for building hope and unity within communities. At the heart of this celebration are the Nguzo Saba, or the seven principles, each embodying values that are essential not only for individual growth but also for the collective upliftment of society. This article delves into how each of these principles contributes to fostering hope and unity.

Umoja (Unity): Building Solidarity and Strength

Umoja, meaning unity, encourages us to strive for and maintain harmony in the family, community, nation, and race. In today's fragmented world, Umoja's emphasis on unity is a beacon of hope, reminding us that our strength lies in our collective spirit and shared humanity.

Kujichagulia (Self-Determination): Empowering Voices

Kujichagulia, or self-determination, is about defining ourselves, naming ourselves, and speaking for ourselves. This principle instills hope by empowering individuals and communities to take charge of their destiny, fostering a sense of agency and responsibility.

Ujima (Collective Work and Responsibility): A Commitment to Each Other

Ujima, translating to collective work and responsibility, reinforces the idea that our fates are intertwined. It cultivates hope by encouraging collective efforts and mutual support, reminding us that we are not alone in our struggles and aspirations.

Ujamaa (Cooperative Economics): Strengthening Communities Economically

Ujamaa emphasizes cooperative economics, urging us to build and maintain our own stores, shops, and businesses. This principle fosters economic resilience and independence, essential for creating hopeful futures in marginalized communities.

Nia (Purpose): Cultivating Meaningful Existence

Nia, or purpose, encourages us to look inward to find our calling and outward to contribute to the community. This principle is a wellspring of hope, as it guides individuals to lead lives filled with intention and positive impact.

Kuumba (Creativity): The Power of Innovation

Kuumba, meaning creativity, pushes us to do as much as we can, in the way we can, to leave our communities more beautiful and beneficial than we inherited them. This principle sparks hope through innovation, driving us to create solutions and envision a better world.

Imani (Faith): Belief in the Heart of the Community

Imani, or faith, is about believing in our people, our educators, our leaders, and the righteousness of our struggle. This principle nurtures hope by fostering a deep-rooted belief in our collective potential and future success.

Conclusion:

The seven principles of Kwanzaa are more than just concepts; they are practical guidelines for building a society imbued with hope and unity. As we embrace these values, we pave the way for a future that is not only prosperous but also deeply connected and harmoniously unified.

PATH BENDER

By: Antonio T. Smith, Jr

HARDCOVER PRICE: $29.99

**FIGHTING FOR MY
LIFE TO WIN (PAPERBACK)**

By: Arshisa Adejiyan

PRICE: $16.99

**OFF THE PATH
(PAPERBACK)**

By: Tierell Goodman

PRICE: $24.99

**RESILIENT SAILING
(PAPERBACK)**

By: Dr Carl M Barnes

PRICE: $28.26

**NATURE'S PHARMACY :
UNLOCKING THE
POWER OF
MEDICINAL HERBS**

By: Deaunna M Smith

PRICE: $32.99

**ARE YOU HAPPY :
FINDING THE CEO
IN YOU (HARDCOVER)**

By: M.L.Ruscsak

PRICE: $29.99

Embracing the Serenity: A moment of mindfulness in the midst of nature, brought to you by Trient Press – nurturing your mindset, one page at a time.

+1 -775-249-7401

info@trientperess.com
www.trientpress.com

www.rennervationfoundation.org/

Lighting the Path:
The RennerVation Foundation's
MISSION OF HOPE AND PURPOSE

In the heart of the festive season, when the spirit of giving and compassion illuminates every corner, the RennerVation Foundation emerges not just as an organization, but as a beacon of hope and inspiration. With its roots deeply planted in the noble ideal of providing resources and support for foster children, at-risk youth, and underserved communities, this philanthropic entity distinguishes itself through its unwavering commitment to nurturing and empowering the next generation.

IMAGE SOURCE: RENNERVATION FPOUNDATION

Founded on the principles of empathy, support, and growth, the RennerVation Foundation has become a symbol of transformative change. It's a place where young dreams are fostered and the seeds of potential are carefully nurtured. The foundation's approach is not just about offering temporary aid; it's about creating sustainable pathways for growth and development, enabling these young individuals to build a foundation of strength and purpose.

As the festive lights twinkle and the air fills with the melody of the season, the RennerVation Foundation's work becomes even more poignant. This is a time when the contrast between abundance and need becomes more visible, and the foundation's efforts shine as a testament to the power of collective compassion and action. By focusing on the holistic development of those they serve, the foundation ensures that the spirit of the season extends beyond the festive period, instilling a lasting impact in the lives of many.

In this time of celebration and reflection, the RennerVation Foundation stands as a reminder of the true essence of the season: giving, not just in terms of material gifts, but giving hope, guidance, and opportunities for a brighter future. Their unique approach to nurturing the next generation is a vital contribution to creating a more inclusive and compassionate world, embodying the very best of the holiday spirit.

A Vision of Empowerment

THE RENNERVATION FOUNDATION, A BEACON OF HOPE IN THIS SEASON OF WARMTH, EMPOWERS FOSTER CHILDREN AND UNDERSERVED YOUTH, EMBODYING THE TRUE SPIRIT OF GIVING AND COMPASSION.

Central to the ethos of the RennerVation Foundation is a vision that is both straightforward and deeply impactful: to bestow upon young lives the tools and opportunities they need to discover and embrace their purpose and joy. This mission transcends the boundaries of mere material assistance; it is about kindling a flame of hope and a sense of boundless possibility in young individuals who may have been marginalized or forgotten by society. The foundation's philosophy is anchored in the belief that every child and youth, regardless of their background, deserves a chance to carve out a fulfilling and meaningful life.

This vision of empowerment involves creating avenues for growth and self-discovery that are tailored to individual needs and aspirations. The foundation recognizes that empowerment is not a one-size-fits-all solution but a personal journey that varies from one individual to another. Whether it's through educational programs, artistic endeavors, or mentorship, the foundation seeks to provide a diverse range of resources that cater to the unique talents and interests of each young person they support. This holistic approach ensures that the assistance provided is not only effective but also resonates on a deeper, more personal level with those it seeks to aid.

Furthermore, at the heart of the RennerVation Foundation's mission is the drive to foster not just individual success but also a sense of community and belonging. By nurturing these young minds, the foundation is not only shaping a brighter future for them but is also actively contributing to the creation of a more inclusive, empathetic, and vibrant society. This vision of empowerment is about lifting others as we climb, ensuring that as these young individuals rise, they also become beacons of hope and inspiration for others in their communities. In this way, the RennerVation Foundation's mission is not just about changing lives; it's about transforming futures.

The Gift of Opportunity

In the festive season, an atmosphere of reflection, gratitude, and generosity envelops us, encouraging us to think beyond ourselves and to consider the impact we have on others. It is in this spirit that the RennerVation Foundation's work becomes particularly resonant. Aligning seamlessly with these seasonal values, the foundation dedicates itself to giving a most precious gift: the gift of opportunity. This commitment is not just about providing temporary aid or relief; it is about opening doors to new possibilities and pathways that can lead to transformative changes in the lives of those they assist.

The opportunities provided by the RennerVation Foundation are manifold and diverse, encompassing creative arts, educational resources, mentorship programs, and more. Each of these avenues offers a unique way for young individuals to explore their talents, develop their skills, and gain the confidence needed to pursue their dreams. For instance, through the creative arts, children and youth find not only an outlet for expression but also a tool for healing and self-discovery. Educational resources, on the other hand, provide the foundational knowledge and critical thinking skills essential in today's world, while mentorship programs connect these young minds with role models and guides who can offer wisdom, support, and real-world insights.

Moreover, the foundation's focus on opportunity is about breaking the cycle of disadvantage and opening up a world where potential is not hindered by circumstance. By equipping these young individuals with the tools they need to succeed, the foundation is actively contributing to leveling the playing field. It recognizes that talent and ambition are universal, but opportunity is not, and strives to bridge this gap. The foundation's efforts in providing these opportunities are akin to planting seeds of possibility in fertile ground, nurturing them to grow, flourish, and eventually bear fruit.

In essence, the RennerVation Foundation's gift of opportunity is a beacon of hope in a world that often seems fraught with challenges. As we embrace the festive season's spirit of giving, the foundation's work stands as a reminder of the profound impact that thoughtful, sustained support can have on the lives of individuals and, by extension, on the broader fabric of society. Their dedication to providing opportunities is not just a gift to the immediate recipients but a contribution to a more hopeful, equitable, and prosperous future for all.

The RennerVation Foundation provides creative, thoughtful and purposeful tools and resources for foster children, at-risk youth, and other underserved communities to encourage them to find...

RennerVation Foundation

A Unique Approach

THE RENNERVATION FOUNDATION DISTINGUISHES ITSELF THROUGH ITS CREATIVE AND THOUGHTFUL APPROACH TO PHILANTHROPY. IT'S AN ORGANIZATION THAT TRANSCENDS THE TRADITIONAL BOUNDS OF RESOURCE PROVISION, DELVING DEEPLY INTO THE UNIQUE AND DIVERSE NEEDS OF THE COMMUNITIES IT SERVES. THIS FOUNDATION UNDERSTANDS THAT EACH CHILD AND YOUNG PERSON IT SUPPORTS IS AN INDIVIDUAL WITH DISTINCT DREAMS, ASPIRATIONS, AND CHALLENGES. BY METICULOUSLY TAILORING THEIR SUPPORT, THE FOUNDATION ENSURES THAT ITS INTERVENTIONS ARE NOT JUST EFFECTIVE BUT DEEPLY RESONANT WITH THE INDIVIDUALS THEY AIM TO UPLIFT.

AT THE RENNERVATION FOUNDATION, IT'S ABOUT MORE THAN JUST MEETING BASIC NEEDS; IT'S ABOUT FOSTERING AN ENVIRONMENT WHERE YOUNG MINDS CAN FLOURISH AND EXPLORE THEIR POTENTIAL. WHETHER IT'S THROUGH EDUCATIONAL PROGRAMS, CREATIVE ARTS WORKSHOPS, OR MENTORSHIP INITIATIVES, THE FOUNDATION'S OFFERINGS ARE DESIGNED TO UNLOCK THE LATENT TALENTS AND ABILITIES IN EACH CHILD. THIS BESPOKE APPROACH EMPOWERS YOUTH TO PURSUE THEIR PASSIONS, DISCOVER THEIR STRENGTHS, AND BUILD CONFIDENCE IN THEIR ABILITIES.

MOREOVER, THE FOUNDATION'S STRATEGY IS GROUNDED IN THE BELIEF THAT PROVIDING RESOURCES IS ONLY PART OF THE SOLUTION. EQUALLY IMPORTANT IS THE CULTIVATION OF SAFE, NURTURING SPACES WHERE YOUNG PEOPLE CAN FEEL VALUED, HEARD, AND INSPIRED. THE RENNERVATION FOUNDATION'S PROGRAMS ARE THEREFORE IMBUED WITH AN ETHOS OF CARE, ENCOURAGEMENT, AND EMPOWERMENT, ENSURING THAT EACH INTERACTION LEAVES A POSITIVE IMPRINT ON THE LIVES OF THESE YOUNG INDIVIDUALS.

THIS NUANCED AND EMPATHETIC APPROACH SETS THE RENNERVATION FOUNDATION APART IN THE LANDSCAPE OF PHILANTHROPIC ORGANIZATIONS. IT'S A TESTAMENT TO THEIR COMMITMENT NOT JUST TO AID BUT TO TRANSFORM LIVES, HELPING TO SHAPE A FUTURE WHERE EVERY CHILD AND YOUNG PERSON CAN ASPIRE TO AND ACHIEVE THEIR OWN VERSION OF SUCCESS. IN DOING SO, THE RENNERVATION FOUNDATION IS NOT JUST CHANGING INDIVIDUAL LIVES; IT IS BUILDING A MORE HOPEFUL, INCLUSIVE, AND VIBRANT FUTURE FOR ALL.

A Call to Action

AS THE HOLIDAY SEASON UNFOLDS, ADORNED WITH ITS FESTIVE SPIRIT AND A SENSE OF COMMUNAL JOY, THE RENNERVATION FOUNDATION STANDS AS A POIGNANT REMINDER OF THE PROFOUND IMPACT OF GIVING BACK. IT EXTENDS A CALL TO ACTION THAT RESONATES BEYOND THE SEASONAL CELEBRATIONS, INVITING EACH OF US TO PLAY A PART IN FOSTERING A BRIGHTER FUTURE. THIS CALL IS NOT JUST ABOUT FINANCIAL CONTRIBUTIONS; IT ENCOMPASSES A WIDE ARRAY OF ACTIONS THAT COLLECTIVELY CONTRIBUTE TO THE NOBLE CAUSE OF THE FOUNDATION. WHETHER IT'S THROUGH DONATIONS, WHICH ARE VITAL FOR THE CONTINUATION OF THEIR PROGRAMS, OR VOLUNTEERING TIME AND SKILLS TO DIRECTLY SUPPORT THEIR INITIATIVES, EVERY CONTRIBUTION MAKES A SIGNIFICANT DIFFERENCE.

THIS CALL TO ACTION ALSO RECOGNIZES THE POWER OF ADVOCACY AND AWARENESS. IN OUR INTERCONNECTED WORLD, SIMPLY SPREADING THE WORD ABOUT THE FOUNDATION'S MISSION CAN HAVE FAR-REACHING EFFECTS. SHARING STORIES OF THE FOUNDATION'S IMPACT ON SOCIAL MEDIA, ENGAGING IN COMMUNITY DISCUSSIONS, OR EVEN INITIATING FUNDRAISERS AND AWARENESS CAMPAIGNS ARE INVALUABLE WAYS TO SUPPORT THEIR CAUSE. THIS FORM OF INVOLVEMENT NOT ONLY AIDS IN RESOURCE ACCUMULATION BUT ALSO HELPS IN BUILDING A COMMUNITY OF LIKE-MINDED INDIVIDUALS, UNITED IN THEIR COMMITMENT TO POSITIVE CHANGE.

FURTHERMORE, THE RENNERVATION FOUNDATION'S CALL TO ACTION IS AN INVITATION TO REFLECT ON THE BROADER IMPLICATIONS OF OUR CONTRIBUTIONS. IT'S AN ENCOURAGEMENT TO THINK ABOUT PHILANTHROPY NOT AS A SEASONAL ACTIVITY BUT AS A LIFELONG COMMITMENT TO EMPATHY AND SOCIAL RESPONSIBILITY. BY RESPONDING TO THIS CALL, WE CONTRIBUTE TO A WORLD WHERE EVERY CHILD, IRRESPECTIVE OF THEIR BACKGROUND, HAS THE OPPORTUNITY TO THRIVE, LEARN, AND GROW. THE FOUNDATION'S VISION OF A WORLD WHERE POTENTIAL IS NURTURED AND DREAMS ARE PURSUED IS A VISION THAT REQUIRES COLLECTIVE EFFORT AND SUSTAINED COMMITMENT. AS WE BASK IN THE WARMTH OF THE HOLIDAY SEASON, LET US EMBRACE THIS CALL TO ACTION WITH OPEN HEARTS AND MINDS, CONTRIBUTING IN WHATEVER WAY WE CAN TO THIS NOBLE ENDEAVOR.

FOUNDATION'S WORK HAS HELPED FOSTER A COMMUNITY ETHOS THAT VALUES AND SUPPORTS EVERY CHILD'S POTENTIAL, CREATING A NURTURING ENVIRONMENT WHERE YOUNG MINDS CAN THRIVE. THIS COLLECTIVE CHANGE IS PERHAPS THE MOST SIGNIFICANT LEGACY OF THE RENNERVATION FOUNDATION – A LEGACY OF EMPOWERED INDIVIDUALS AND STRENGTHENED COMMUNITIES, EACH STORY A THREAD IN THE EVER-GROWING TAPESTRY OF SUCCESS AND TRANSFORMATION.

December Reflections: Embracing the End as a New Beginning

Introduction:

December, the final chapter of the year, often brings a mix of reflection and anticipation. As the days grow shorter and the nights longer, we are reminded of the cyclical nature of life. This month, traditionally a time of festivity and celebration, also provides us with a unique opportunity to pause, reflect, and prepare for the new beginnings that lie ahead.

The Power of Reflection:

December invites us to look back on the year that has passed. It's a time to celebrate our triumphs, learn from our challenges, and express gratitude for the journey. Each experience, whether joyous or difficult, has contributed to our growth and understanding. Reflecting on these moments allows us to gain perspective, appreciate our resilience, and acknowledge the progress we've made.

Embracing the Present:

While reflection is vital, December also teaches us the importance of being present. Amid the holiday rush, it's essential to find moments of stillness and peace. Mindfulness in our daily activities – whether it's decorating our homes, preparing meals, or spending time with loved ones – can transform routine actions into joyful celebrations of the now.

Preparing for New Beginnings:

As December closes the year, it also ushers in the promise of a new start. This transition is a powerful reminder that endings are also beginnings. Setting intentions for the coming year, rather than rigid resolutions, can be a more compassionate and flexible approach to personal growth. It's about aligning our aspirations with our core values and being open to the journey ahead, with all its potential and possibility.

A Message of Hope and Unity:

December's festive spirit, regardless of cultural or religious background, echoes a universal message of hope and unity. It's a time to come together, celebrate our shared humanity, and spread kindness and goodwill. In a world that can often feel divided, this month reminds us of the power of community and the strength found in our collective spirit.

Conclusion:

As we navigate the final days of December, let us carry its lessons into the new year. By reflecting on our past, being present in our today, and looking forward with hope, we can step into the future with renewed energy and optimism. December is not just an end, but a beacon of new beginnings, filled with endless possibilities and opportunities for growth.

MINDSET MOMENTS

PRESENTS

Sacred Symbols: The Star of Bethlehem

In the tapestry of history, few symbols hold as much mystery and wonder as the Star of Bethlehem. Revered in many cultures and central to the Christmas narrative, this celestial phenomenon has captivated scholars, theologians, and astronomers for centuries. As we delve into the story of the Star of Bethlehem, we unravel a narrative rich in symbolism, faith, and astronomical intrigue.

The Story of the Star of Bethlehem

The enigmatic tale of the Star of Bethlehem, also revered as the Christmas Star, finds its origins in the Gospel of Matthew in the Christian Bible. This celestial symbol is described as heralding the birth of Jesus Christ, serving as a guide to the Magi, or Wise Men, on their journey to Bethlehem. Over centuries, this singular star has evolved into a profound emblem of guidance, hope, and the dawn of new beginnings. Its significance has been captured in an array of artistic expressions, from Renaissance paintings to modern-day carols, transcending its biblical roots to resonate with a universal message of enlightenment and renewal.

This star, set against the backdrop of a nocturnal sky, has been a source of fascination and inspiration. It is often depicted as shining more brightly than its celestial counterparts, a beacon of light in the darkness, leading the way to a significant revelation. Its representation in art and culture often sees it as a luminous, guiding presence, symbolizing the journey each individual undertakes in search of truth and understanding.

Theories and Interpretations

The true nature of the Star of Bethlehem has been a subject of enduring intrigue and scholarly debate. Astronomers and historians have speculated various astronomical phenomena that could explain its appearance. Was it a supernova, an exploding star that briefly outshines entire galaxies? Or perhaps a comet, with its icy core and luminous tail, gracing the ancient skies? Another theory posits a rare conjunction of planets, where celestial bodies align to create a striking visual spectacle. Each of these theories offers a different lens through which to view this historical event, intertwining the narrative with cosmic occurrences.

Some scholars and theologians, however, view the star as a miraculous event, one that defies astronomical categorization. In this perspective, the star is seen as a divine sign, an intervention by a higher power to mark a momentous event in human history. This interpretation adds a layer of mystical significance to the star, inviting believers to see it as a direct communication from the divine.

This pursuit to understand the Star of Bethlehem does more than satisfy historical curiosity; it represents a unique confluence of faith and science. On one hand, astronomers delve into the past, seeking evidence in the alignments and movements of stars and planets. On the other, theologians and believers look to the symbolism and spiritual meaning behind this celestial event. This juxtaposition of scientific inquiry and faith-based interpretation lends a rich complexity to the star's symbolism, making it a subject of wonder, debate, and inspiration across diverse fields of study.

In essence, the Star of Bethlehem, whether a miraculous sign or an extraordinary astronomical event, remains a powerful symbol. It captures the human quest for meaning, the search for light in the darkness, and the desire to understand our place in the grand tapestry of the universe. Its story, nestled within ancient texts, continues to spark imagination and exploration, inviting us to look up and wonder.

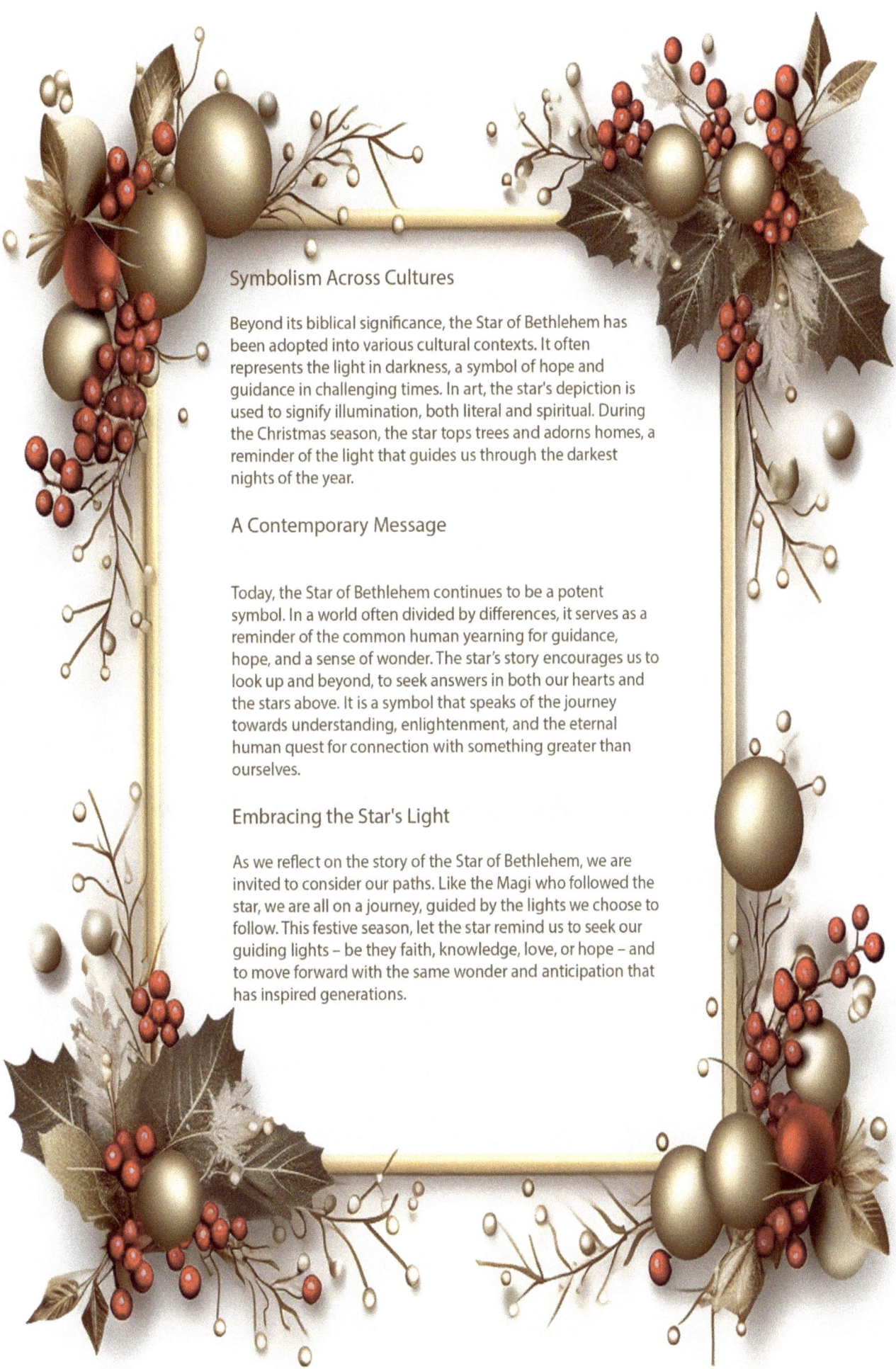

Symbolism Across Cultures

Beyond its biblical significance, the Star of Bethlehem has been adopted into various cultural contexts. It often represents the light in darkness, a symbol of hope and guidance in challenging times. In art, the star's depiction is used to signify illumination, both literal and spiritual. During the Christmas season, the star tops trees and adorns homes, a reminder of the light that guides us through the darkest nights of the year.

A Contemporary Message

Today, the Star of Bethlehem continues to be a potent symbol. In a world often divided by differences, it serves as a reminder of the common human yearning for guidance, hope, and a sense of wonder. The star's story encourages us to look up and beyond, to seek answers in both our hearts and the stars above. It is a symbol that speaks of the journey towards understanding, enlightenment, and the eternal human quest for connection with something greater than ourselves.

Embracing the Star's Light

As we reflect on the story of the Star of Bethlehem, we are invited to consider our paths. Like the Magi who followed the star, we are all on a journey, guided by the lights we choose to follow. This festive season, let the star remind us to seek our guiding lights – be they faith, knowledge, love, or hope – and to move forward with the same wonder and anticipation that has inspired generations.

The Art of Giving:

Philanthropic Movements Making a Difference This Holiday Season

As the holiday season wraps the world in a blanket of shimmering lights and joyous melodies, a different kind of illumination takes place – one that emanates from the heart of philanthropy. Across the globe, charitable organizations and philanthropic movements are igniting sparks of hope and compassion, embodying the true spirit of the season. This story delves into the diverse and impactful efforts of these groups, showcasing how their work is transforming lives and strengthening communities during this time of giving.

Warmth in Winter: The Blanket and Coat Drive

As the cold tendrils of winter weave their way through cities and towns, the Blanket and Coat Drive stands as a beacon of warmth and humanity. This initiative, born out of a deep understanding of the challenges faced by the homeless and underprivileged during the colder months, takes on the crucial task of collecting and distributing essential winter wear. The drive symbolizes more than just physical warmth; it's a manifestation of communal care and empathy.

Volunteers, the lifeblood of this drive, work tirelessly, often braving the cold themselves as they traverse through streets and shelters. They are on a mission to ensure that no one is left vulnerable to the harsh winter elements. These volunteers, armed with blankets and coats, are not just distributing winter wear; they are wrapping individuals in a metaphorical embrace, offering comfort and reassurance.

The impact of this initiative is profound. Each blanket and coat becomes a tangible symbol of care and solidarity, silently conveying to the recipients that they are seen and valued, even in their most vulnerable moments. This gesture of kindness often becomes a source of emotional warmth, kindling a sense of hope and belonging in the hearts of those who find themselves on the fringes of society during these cold months.

The Gift of Learning: Educational Sponsorship Programs

In parallel to the efforts to provide physical warmth, the spirit of the holiday season is further exemplified in the realm of education. Educational Sponsorship Programs emerge as pivotal players in transforming the lives of young individuals in underprivileged communities. These programs do more than just alleviate financial burdens; they unlock doors to new worlds of knowledge and opportunity.

Through scholarships and the provision of educational resources, these programs are actively dismantling the barriers that often keep education out of reach for many. Beyond the financial support, the mentorship and guidance offered by these programs play a crucial role. They not only illuminate academic paths but also nurture the personal growth of each student.

As students engage with these educational opportunities, they embark on a journey of self-discovery and development. The impact of these programs is far-reaching, extending beyond the individual beneficiaries. As these young minds are nurtured, they become agents of change within their communities, driving a cycle of learning, growth, and community upliftment. The ripple effect of these educational sponsorships is seen in the strengthened fabric of entire communities, where education becomes a shared value and a collective goal.

Healing Through Giving: Healthcare Access Initiatives

The holiday season, with its ethos of generosity and compassion, finds a profound reflection in the efforts of Healthcare Access Initiatives. These initiatives are dedicated to bridging the healthcare gap, ensuring that medical care is a universal right, not a privilege. Their work gains additional significance during the holiday season, a time that can amplify health challenges for many. Through services like free health clinics and mobile medical units, these initiatives ensure that essential healthcare reaches those who need it most.

In various communities, these healthcare programs become more than just service providers; they are lifelines. They offer much-needed medical relief to individuals and families who, without this support, would face the cold season in vulnerability and uncertainty. The presence of these healthcare services in underserved areas is a reassuring sign of a community's commitment to its members, particularly the most vulnerable.

Moreover, these initiatives are staffed by selfless healthcare professionals and volunteers who work tirelessly. Their dedication goes beyond the call of duty, often providing care under challenging circumstances. This commitment is a testament to the human spirit's capacity for empathy and service, particularly during times of celebration and reflection like the holidays.

A Canvas of Compassion: The Arts and Community Engagement

Parallel to the strides made in healthcare, the realm of art emerges as a powerful tool for community engagement and healing. Philanthropic groups focusing on the arts are creating avenues for expression and connection, particularly among underprivileged youth and marginalized groups. These initiatives supply art materials, conduct workshops, and organize exhibitions, transforming community spaces into hubs of creativity and sharing.

Art, in these settings, becomes more than just a medium for expression; it serves as a therapeutic tool and a means of forging connections. Individuals who participate in these programs find not only an outlet for their emotions and experiences but also a way to connect with others within their community. The process of creating art becomes a journey of self-discovery and mutual understanding.

The culmination of these artistic endeavors often takes place in holiday exhibitions, where the artworks are displayed. These exhibitions are vibrant celebrations of human resilience and creativity, showcasing the power of art to transcend barriers and bring people together. The displayed works are not just pieces of art; they are stories of individual journeys and collective experiences, each canvas or sculpture echoing the spirit of the community that created it.

Conclusion: The Ripple Effect of Giving

As we reflect on the impact of these philanthropic movements, it becomes evident that the essence of the holiday season extends far beyond the exchange of material gifts. It's about the ripples of change, kindness, and connection that these initiatives foster. The efforts of Healthcare Access Initiatives and Arts and Community Engagement programs exemplify the true spirit of giving - a spirit that encompasses empathy, care, and the building of inclusive communities.

December Affirmations

"I embrace the peace and joy of the holiday season with an open heart."

"Every day in December, I find moments of gratitude and happiness."

"I am surrounded by love, light, and the warmth of the holiday spirit."

"This month, I choose to focus on the positives and cherish every moment."

"I am a beacon of hope and kindness in this festive season."

"I welcome the end of the year with reflection and a sense of accomplishment."

"My heart is open to giving and receiving love during this holiday season."

"I am grateful for the year's lessons and ready for new beginnings."

"December's chill is a reminder of the warmth and comfort in my life."

"I am at peace with the past year and look forward to what's ahead."

"This holiday season, I find joy in small things and big celebrations alike."

"I am worthy of rest, relaxation, and rejuvenation this December."

"I spread cheer and positivity wherever I go this month."

"I embrace the spirit of giving and share my blessings with others."

"My end-of-year reflections are filled with gratitude and hope."

"I am patient and kind to myself and others during the holiday hustle."

"This December, I am a shining example of generosity and goodwill."

"I welcome the winter's beauty with awe and appreciation."

"Each day of this month brings new opportunities for joy and connection."

"I am confident and calm as I prepare for the new year."

"The festive lights of December brighten my mood and outlook."

"I am in harmony with the season's pace – slowing down when needed."

"I cherish the traditions and memories that make this month special."

UNLEASH YOUR TRUE BEAUTY WITH MICABEAUTY - WHERE EVERY SHADE IS CELEBRATED!

Discover Your Perfect Match: Dive into the world of MicaBeauty, where we embrace every skin tone with our inclusive and personalized beauty range. From radiant foundations to luscious lip balms, our non-toxic, harsh chemical-free products are crafted for your unique beauty.

Be Part of Our Story: Join us on a journey of beauty that defies norms. At MicaBeauty, we're more than just a brand; we're a community that celebrates the real you.

https://shrsl.com/4cp62

🏠 > TapJoy - Mica Beauty Cosmetics & Skincare Products

GLOW GETTER VALUE KIT

$175.00 ~~$210.00~~

or 4 interest-free payments of $43.75 with 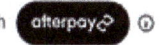 ⓘ

6-piece full size skincare products + mini fridge

Note: Kits are not available internationally

Special Offer: Enjoy free shipping on U.S. orders over $50! Plus, get a FREE mini fridge with purchases over $100*

Mindset Moments

Festive Innovations: Sustainable and Eco-Friendly Holiday Practices

In a quaint, picturesque town nestled in the heart of the mountains, the holiday season was blooming in a most extraordinary way. This year, the town's residents decided to embrace the festive spirit with a sustainable twist, sparking a wave of innovative, eco-friendly celebrations that captured the imagination of young and old alike.

A Green Beginning

It all started with a community meeting, where the townspeople gathered to brainstorm ideas for a more environmentally conscious holiday season. Sarah, a local school teacher, suggested using natural materials for decorations. Inspired, the community set out to transform the town into a green winter wonderland.

Nature's Decor

The town square, usually adorned with plastic ornaments and synthetic tinsel, was transformed using biodegradable and recyclable materials. Families gathered pine cones, autumn leaves, and branches, turning them into beautiful garlands and wreaths. Children crafted ornaments from clay and painted them with natural dyes, their laughter echoing through the streets as they worked together to decorate the community Christmas tree, a living tree that had been part of the square for decades.

Conscious Gifting

Gift-giving, a central tradition of the holiday season, was reimagined. The townspeople organized a gift exchange where the focus was on handmade, second-hand, or locally sourced gifts. John, the town carpenter, crafted wooden toys for the children, while Mary, the local seamstress, sewed quilts and scarves from upcycled fabrics. The town's bakery prepared gift baskets filled with organic, home-baked treats.

Festive Feasts with a Purpose

The holiday feasts, too, saw a transformation. Community potlucks replaced the usual lavish parties, with a focus on locally sourced, organic ingredients. The town's farmers provided fresh vegetables and fruits, while the local grocer offered bulk bins to reduce packaging waste. The festive tables were a mosaic of homemade dishes, each telling a story of tradition, care, and sustainability.

Mindset Moments

As the initiative gained momentum, the residents introduced another eco-friendly practice: candlelit evenings. This tradition quickly became a cherished part of the town's holiday celebrations. On select evenings, as dusk fell, families and neighbors would gather, lighting candles that cast a warm, serene glow over their gatherings. These candlelit events, often accompanied by acoustic music and storytelling, offered a return to simpler joys and provided a stark contrast to the usual bright and bustling holiday lights. The flickering candlelight added an intimate and reflective quality to the celebrations, encouraging people to slow down and savor the moment.

This shift towards more sustainable lighting practices not only reduced the town's carbon footprint but also fostered a deeper sense of community. The soft illumination of solar lights and candles brought people closer together, both literally and metaphorically, as they shared in the beauty of a less commercial, more mindful holiday experience. The town's initiative in lighting the way with eco-friendly practices became a shining example of how small changes could create a significant impact, not just environmentally, but also in enhancing the warmth and spirit of the holiday season.

Lighting the Way

In the heart of the town's transformation towards a sustainable holiday season, even the quintessential twinkling lights received an eco-conscious makeover. The townspeople, driven by their commitment to the environment, decided to replace the traditional electric holiday lights with solar-powered alternatives. This innovative approach not only reduced the town's energy consumption but also brought a new dimension to the festive decorations. The streets and homes were adorned with these solar lights, which captured the sun's energy during the day and transformed it into a soft, ambient glow at night, creating a magical atmosphere that was both beautiful and sustainable.

Spreading the Message

The town's eco-friendly holiday spirit attracted attention far and wide. Visitors came to witness this green revolution, taking with them ideas and inspiration. Local schools organized workshops on sustainable practices, and the town's initiative was featured in regional news, spreading the message of an environmentally conscious holiday.

A Lasting Impact

As the holiday season drew to a close, the residents of the town realized that their efforts had kindled a deeper change. What started as a festive experiment had blossomed into a community-wide commitment to sustainability. The eco-friendly practices, initially meant for the holidays, became a part of everyday life, turning the town into a beacon of environmental responsibility.

This inspiring story of a small town's journey towards a sustainable holiday season serves as a reminder of the impact collective action can have. It shows how tradition and innovation can intertwine to create a celebration that honors both the spirit of the season and the well-being of our planet.

Embracing Resilience:
A Mindset Shift in the Face of Challenges

Life is a series of peaks and valleys, and our ability to navigate these challenges often hinges on our mindset. Resilience, the unwavering determination to bounce back from adversity, is a powerful mindset that can transform setbacks into stepping stones for personal growth. In the face of life's inevitable challenges, adopting a resilient mindset becomes not just an option but a key to unlocking our true potential.

The Power of Perspective: Resilience starts with a shift in perspective. Instead of viewing challenges as insurmountable roadblocks, consider them as opportunities for growth and learning. Embracing a mindset that sees setbacks as temporary and solvable opens the door to creative problem-solving and personal development.

Learning from Adversity: Think of resilience as a muscle that strengthens with each challenge. Every setback provides an opportunity to learn more about ourselves, our strengths, and areas for improvement. By reflecting on the lessons embedded in difficult experiences, we can cultivate a resilient mindset that turns adversity into a source of wisdom.

The Role of Positive Self-Talk: Our inner dialogue shapes our reality. When faced with challenges, practicing positive self-talk can be a game-changer. Replace self-doubt with affirmations that reinforce your abilities and strengths. By consciously choosing empowering thoughts, you lay the foundation for a resilient mindset that propels you forward.

Building a Support Network: Resilience is not a solitary journey. Cultivate a support network of friends, family, and mentors who can provide guidance and encouragement during tough times. Sharing experiences and seeking support not only strengthens your resilience but also fosters a sense of connection and belonging.

As you navigate the unpredictable journey of life, remember that resilience is a skill you can cultivate. Embrace challenges as opportunities for growth, learn from adversity, practice positive self-talk, and build a strong support network. By adopting a resilient mindset, you not only navigate challenges more effectively but also emerge stronger on the other side.

Resilience is not about avoiding challenges but about facing them head-on with courage and a positive mindset. As you encounter obstacles on your journey, let resilience be your compass, guiding you toward growth and self-discovery. Embrace the power of resilience, and watch how challenges transform from roadblocks into stepping stones toward a more fulfilling life.

Written By :
Renea Linsom

Deaunna Marie
The Holistic Visionary of Our Times

In a world increasingly seeking balance and wellness, Deaunna Marie emerges as a beacon of hope and transformation. As a certified herbalist and the architect of the "Always Becoming" philosophy, Deaunna's unique approach to holistic health is not just about healing the body, but also about nurturing the mind and spirit.

The Philosophy of "Always Becoming":
Deaunna's "Always Becoming" philosophy encompasses 46 pioneering principles, each a testament to her belief in continuous growth and transformation. This philosophy is rooted in the understanding that wellness is a dynamic journey, not a static state. It invites individuals to embrace change, explore the depths of their being, and cultivate a harmonious balance between their physical, emotional, and spiritual dimensions..

A Visionary's Path:
Deaunna Marie's path to becoming a holistic luminary was carved through years of study and personal exploration. Her journey into herbalism and natural remedies was fueled by a passion for understanding the intricate connections between nature and human health. This quest for knowledge led her to develop innovative approaches to holistic well-being that resonate deeply with those seeking a more integrative way of living..

The Impact of Her Work:
Deaunna's influence extends beyond individual wellness. Through her workshops, speaking engagements, and writings, she has created a community of like-minded individuals who are collectively exploring the frontiers of holistic health. Her work encourages a shift from traditional paradigms of health care towards more inclusive, empathetic, and nature-aligned practices.

Looking Forward:
As Deaunna Marie continues to expand her horizons, she remains committed to her mission of guiding others on their path to holistic wellness. Her future endeavors, no doubt, will continue to inspire and empower individuals to embrace their journey of "Always Becoming," fostering a world where holistic health is not just an aspiration, but a lived reality..

Illuminating Leadership:

Deaunna Marie's Framework of Hope

Fostering Hope through Holistic Leadership:
Deaunna Marie's leadership style is a radiant example of hope in action. In a world often clouded by uncertainty and discord, she stands as a luminary, guiding individuals towards a future filled with possibility and wellness. Her leadership transcends the boundaries of conventional health advocacy, embodying a holistic approach that intertwines the physical, emotional, and spiritual well-being of her community.

The Role of Hope in Healing:
Central to Deaunna's philosophy is the belief that hope is a powerful catalyst for healing. She understands that the journey to wellness is not just about overcoming physical ailments but also about nurturing a positive mindset. Hope, in her vision, is the cornerstone of resilience and transformation. It encourages individuals to look beyond their current circumstances and envision a healthier, more harmonious life.

Empowering Communities with Optimism:
Deaunna's approach to leadership is deeply rooted in the empowerment of communities. She inspires her followers not just to dream of a better future but to actively participate in creating it. Her workshops and teachings are infused with optimism, encouraging participants to embrace their power to effect change, both in their personal lives and in the broader context of societal well-being.

A Beacon of Change:
As a visionary leader, Deaunna Marie is more than a health advocate; she is a beacon of change. Her framework of hope challenges the status quo and opens up new pathways for communal and individual growth. In a world often starved for positive leadership, her voice resonates with clarity and purpose, guiding many towards a brighter, more hopeful future.

Latkes (Potato Pancakes)

Ingredients:

- 2 pounds of russet potatoes (about 4-5 medium potatoes)
- 1 medium onion
- 2 large eggs
- 1/2 cup all-purpose flour (or matzo meal for a Passover-friendly version)
- 1 teaspoon salt
- 1/2 teaspoon baking powder
- 1/4 teaspoon black pepper
- Vegetable oil for frying

Optional for Serving:
- Applesauce
- Sour cream

Instructions:

Prepare the Potatoes and Onion:
Peel the potatoes and onion. Grate them using the large holes of a box grater or a food processor fitted with a grating disk.

Drain the Mixture:
Place the grated potato and onion mixture in a clean dish towel or cheesecloth. Squeeze out as much liquid as possible into a bowl. Let the liquid sit for a few minutes; the potato starch will settle at the bottom.

Mix the Batter:
In a separate bowl, beat the eggs. Add the flour (or matzo meal), salt, baking powder, and black pepper to the eggs and mix well. Retrieve the potato starch from the bottom of the bowl of potato liquid and add it to the egg mixture. Then, add the drained potato and onion mixture to the bowl. Stir everything together until well combined.

Heat the Oil:
In a large skillet, heat about 1/4 inch of vegetable oil over medium-high heat. The oil is ready when a small amount of the batter sizzles upon contact.

Cook the Latkes:
Drop heaping tablespoons of the potato mixture into the oil, flattening them with the back of the spoon to form pancakes. Be careful not to overcrowd the pan. Fry until the edges are golden brown and crispy, about 3-4 minutes, then flip and cook the other side.

Drain and Serve:
Once the latkes are golden brown on both sides, remove them from the skillet and drain on a paper towel-lined plate. Serve hot with a side of applesauce or sour cream.

Tips:

Keeping the latkes warm: Place cooked latkes in a warm oven (200°F) on a baking sheet lined with paper towels while frying the rest.

For extra crispy latkes, ensure you squeeze out as much liquid as possible from the potato and onion mixture.

These latkes are a delicious and traditional part of Hanukkah celebrations, symbolizing the miracle of the oil in the Hanukkah story. Enjoy them as a tasty treat during the festive season!

Jollof Rice Recipe

Ingredients:

- 2 cups long-grain parboiled rice
- 1/4 cup vegetable oil
- 1 large onion, finely chopped
- 4 cloves garlic, minced
- 1 red bell pepper, chopped
- 1 green bell pepper, chopped
- 1 can (14 oz) crushed tomatoes
- 2 tablespoons tomato paste
- 2 teaspoons curry powder
- 1 teaspoon thyme
- 1/2 teaspoon cayenne pepper (adjust to taste)
- 4 cups chicken or vegetable broth
- Salt and pepper to taste

Optional: cooked chicken, fish, or mixed vegetables for serving

Instructions:

Prepare the Rice:
Rinse the rice under cold water until the water runs clear. Drain and set aside.

Cook the Base:
In a large pot, heat the vegetable oil over medium heat. Add the chopped onions and garlic, cooking until the onions are translucent.

Add the chopped red and green bell peppers and cook for another 3-4 minutes.

Add Tomatoes and Spices:
Stir in the crushed tomatoes, tomato paste, curry powder, thyme, and cayenne pepper. Cook for about 5 minutes, stirring occasionally, until the mixture thickens slightly.

Add the Rice and Broth:
Add the rinsed rice to the pot and stir to coat it with the tomato mixture.

Pour in the chicken or vegetable broth. Bring the mixture to a boil, then reduce the heat to low, cover, and simmer for 20-30 minutes, or until the rice is cooked through and the liquid is absorbed. Stir occasionally to prevent sticking.

Adjust Seasoning:
Taste and adjust the seasoning with salt and pepper as needed.

Serve:
Once the rice is cooked, remove from heat and let it sit for a few minutes. Fluff the rice with a fork before serving.

Optionally, you can serve the Jollof Rice with cooked chicken, fish, or mixed vegetables.

Tips:

The key to great Jollof Rice is in the simmering. It allows the flavors to meld and the rice to absorb the tangy, spicy tomato sauce.

The dish is known for its vibrant red color, which comes from the combination of tomatoes and tomato paste.

Jollof Rice is not only a delicious dish but also a symbol of shared African heritage and is perfect for Kwanzaa celebrations, embodying the holiday's focus on unity and cultural reflection. Enjoy this hearty and flavorful dish with friends and family!

Roast Turkey with Stuffing Recipe

Ingredients:

For the Turkey:
- 1 whole turkey (about 12-14 pounds), thawed if frozen
- 1/4 cup unsalted butter, softened
- Salt and pepper to taste
- Fresh herbs (like rosemary, thyme, and sage)
- 2 onions, quartered
- 2 carrots, cut into large chunks
- 2 celery stalks, cut into large chunks

For the Stuffing:
- 1 loaf day-old bread, cut into cubes (about 10-12 cups)
- 1/2 cup unsalted butter
- 1 large onion, finely chopped
- 2-3 celery stalks, chopped
- 2-3 garlic cloves, minced
- 1 teaspoon dried sage
- 1 teaspoon dried thyme
- 1/2 teaspoon salt
- 1/2 teaspoon black pepper
- 2-3 cups chicken or turkey broth
- 2 eggs, beaten

Instructions:

Prepare the Stuffing:
Preheat the oven to 350°F (175°C).

In a large skillet, melt the butter over medium heat. Add the onion, celery, and garlic, and cook until soft.

In a large bowl, combine the bread cubes with the cooked onion mixture, sage, thyme, salt, and pepper. Stir in the chicken broth and beaten eggs until well mixed. The stuffing should be moist but not soggy. Adjust the amount of broth as needed.

Prepare the Turkey:
Increase the oven temperature to 425°F (220°C).

Pat the turkey dry with paper towels. Rub the entire turkey with softened butter, and then season it inside and out with salt and pepper.

Stuff the turkey cavity with the prepared stuffing, being careful not to pack it too tightly.

Place the turkey breast-side up in a large roasting pan. Tuck the wings under the body. If desired, tie the legs together with kitchen twine.

Surround the turkey with the quartered onions, carrots, and celery stalks.

Roast the Turkey:
Roast the turkey at 425°F (220°C) for about 30 minutes. Then, reduce the oven temperature to 350°F (175°C).

Continue roasting, basting the turkey every 45 minutes with the pan juices. The total cooking time will be about 13 minutes per pound, or until a meat thermometer inserted into the thickest part of the thigh reads 165°F (75°C).

Rest and Serve:
Once cooked, remove the turkey from the oven. Let it rest for about 20-30 minutes before carving. This allows the juices to redistribute, ensuring a moist turkey.

Carve the turkey and serve it with the stuffing and your choice of sides.

Tips:
For safety, it's recommended to cook stuffing separately in a baking dish. However, if you prefer traditional stuffed turkey, ensure the stuffing reaches 165°F (75°C).

Keep an eye on the turkey as it roasts. If the skin browns too quickly, tent it with aluminum foil.

This Roast Turkey with Stuffing recipe is sure to be a delightful centerpiece at your Christmas feast, embodying the warmth and joy of the holiday season!

www.ingramcontent.com/pod-product-compliance
Lightning Source LLC
LaVergne TN
LVHW070540070526
838199LV00076B/6817